Friends With the Moon

Friends With the Moon

☾

Friends With the Moon

☾

Written by Hannah A. Barnette

Friends With the Moon

☾

Friends With the Moon

5

☾

Friends With the Moon

☾

Friends With the Moon

☽

To my dearest sister and my
very best friend.

Friends With the

Moon

☾

Friends With the

Moon

☾

I Made You Into Art

Friends With the Moon

☾

Our eyes meet, and every
heartbeat is a bomb dropping
in my chest—
Love is war.
When our lips converge, a
war ends somewhere—
Love is peace.
Your hands run down my
spine, like you're painting
the Sistine Chapel—
Love is an art.
Our hearts beat in such
synchronicity:

Friends With the Moon

☾

The excitation of atoms—
Love is fatal chemistry.

Friends With the Moon

☾

You look like art.
You are, by far, the most
captivating formation of
atoms I've yet to meet eyes
with.
An original—a priceless
piece of work.
How I hope to spend the rest
of my life in your company,
as if I am bound by grand
museum walls...
Astonished by your soul like
strokes on a canvas.

Friends With the Moon

☾

He says he's a mess, but his
mess is mine.
Whatever is his, I'll share
wholeheartedly.
Whether it be
warfare or red wine,
Wet eyes or bare skin,
Morning breath or the sweet
sin
that follows.
I tell him,
"Honey, you're soul food.

Friends With the Moon

☾

Not that sweet, cheap,
skin-deep shit."
My baby's as deep as the sea
and his soul is as big as they
get.
You told me this would've
been much easier had I been
a bad kisser;
Well I'm not sorry, and I
won't ever be.
'Til your last day, I hope
you're still falling over me.

Friends With the Moon

☾

We stumbled over love like
quicksand—
So take my hand,
and we'll see how deep we
can sink.

Friends With the Moon

☾

I'm afraid there is not,
And nor will there ever be,
Anything that compares
To the nights we spent,
entwined
In the blackness of your
bedroom;
The absence of sight
Heightening the feeling of
our bare skin, coexisting,
And the sound of your soft
breath warming the pit of my
neck.

Friends With the Moon

☾

I am thankful to have always
savored the few minutes
before
Muffled chimes of the train
sang us into the most
peaceful of sleeps.

Friends With the Moon

☾

I'm not religious, but he
makes a woman want to drop
to her knees.
A man like that will have you
thanking the Gods every day
for hand-crafting such a
beautifully twisted and
captivating mind.
Oh honey, you make me want
to pray —
Pray you've found your home
in me and forever you'll stay.
-Heaven Sent

Friends With the Moon

☾

I have loved you in every

color, my dear.

Every

Last

One

Friends With the Moon

☾

I remember a time when I
nearly drowned: It was a
lighted morning in your
kitchen, while gazing deeply
into those hazel eyes.
What a way to go that would
have been.

Friends With the

Moon

☾

Our eyes meet, and the
entirety of me is paralyzed
for a brief second—
The calm before the storm.

Friends With the Moon

☽

I like how I bring out the
lines in your cheeks.
Every time you smile with
those hazel eyes, my knees
get weak.
I might just have to tape my
mouth,
To keep the "I love you"s
from slipping out.
I'm eager to study every inch
of that beautiful mind,
And how perfectly the two of
ours collide.

Friends With the

Moon

☾

A man with an old soul and a
brilliant mind.
He finds much comfort in
black and white, and
definitive answers;
But I've seen you dream in
colors many times.
I've caught glimpses over the
years of your imagination
running wild, and the way
you glow when you smile
with your eyes nearly shut.

Friends With the Moon

☽

Many nights we've drowned
in laughter together and we,
too, have debated the
meanings of life.
I remember the night I asked
you about investing in the
stock market, to which you
responded:

"It's easy, you just have to go
into it not expecting
anything and you'll always
come out on top."

Friends With the Moon

☾

I find it funny that I could
answer your later question
regarding love with the exact
same response. I exist in the
clouds with abstract things,
and you are grounded by
numbers and logic; and
somehow, we still meet—

Somewhere in the middle.

Friends With the Moon

☾

The most beautiful exchange
of words always lies in the
meeting of eyes.

Friends With the Moon

☾

I love you so—
I'll make sure your soul lives
on forever.
I'll make you into art, and,
for years after you've gone,
they will read about your
brilliant mind and your
inescapable charm.

Friends With the

Moon

☾

I hope you bask in the rays
every lovely summer's day,
With a grin hanging on your
face.
As if I *am* the sunshine
beaming down on your
smitten cheeks;
I sun-kissed them quite
nicely.
And when the sun
illuminates every detail in
the clouds, painting a
masterpiece in the sky as she

Friends With the Moon

☾

bids her bittersweet

farewell—

I hope you remember me all

the same, on the day you last

saw my face.

Friends With the

Moon

☾

I see poetry in everything you
do—even in the way you
light up a cigarette.
And the way that crooked
smile hangs on your face
Reminds me of a picture
hanging on the wall of an
old, favorite diner.
When I'm in your presence, I
feel like I'm living out a
novel—because you're one of
those rare, captivating people

Friends With the

Moon

☽

who stand out in mere words

on pages.

I don't write novels, but I'll

write about you—because a

soul like yours deserves to

live on in works of art.

Friends With the

Moon

☾

I didn't want to write poetry
about you.
I thought we were just two
fools doing the things fools
do.
But now your eyes swallow
me whole—
I'm Swimming in your ocean
of blues.
Our lips converge naturally
in the morning, like grass
and dew.

Friends With the Moon

☾

Tangled up in a sea of silk
sheets,
And When I leave my mind's
tangled up with the thoughts
of you.

Friends With the

Moon

☾

My name sounds so different
when it's uttered by your
mouth.
Dripping so smoothly off
your tongue
like sweet, golden honey.
And what am I to do but feel
like I'm a honey bee?

Friends With the Moon

((

It's early, and it's silent.
The rest of the world is
asleep, and my heart is at
ease.
Just your golden eyes, your
sweet smile, and a cup of
black coffee.

Friends With the Moon

☾

I only love madly,
Irrationally;
For I know of no other way
to do so.

Friends With the Moon

☽

I spend most days dreaming
up metaphors to describe the
likes of you, but my words
always seem to fall short.
Always.

Friends With the

Moon

☾

I still remember the look on
your face, when I first
exposed the work of art
which is my body.
A carefully constructed piece
Which took years to break
down and build up a
thousand times.
And even so —
When you saw walls come
tumbling down

Friends With the Moon

☾

With every inch of my mind
and the seams that barely
hold it together,
It was as if the gates of
heaven had surely opened
And no shell of mine could
possibly compare.

Friends With the Moon

☾

I met you only a month ago.
How is it that I already know
your soul?
The truth is, it nearly
swallowed me whole.
I hope the lines in your
cheeks grow deep from
smiling at me, as we grow
old.

Friends With the Moon

☾

I want a vintage love.
A love that's like
blowing the dust off an old,
favorite record.
And no matter how many
times the needle slips out of
my grasp,
The music curves up my lip
ends and makes off with my
heart the same way it did the
first time I listened
to that sweet, familiar tune.

Friends With the

Moon

☾

I want an old soul that stirs

mine —

endlessly.

Friends With the Moon

☾

Friends With the Moon

☾

Soft, but not Sweet

Friends With the Moon

☾

Most men are afraid of me.
I'm jaded, but it's
invigorating if you stay.
I scare off the weak and
shallow 'cause I'm too dark
and too deep—
Full of dimensions;
More than a pretty image.
And if you admire for too
long, you'll find
That you've turned to stone.
-Medusa

Friends With the Moon

☾

He's a good, bad man—
An angel in the daytime
and a fallen angel with the
lights off.
When I'm wrapped up in his
bedsheets,
it's heaven and it's hell.

Friends With the Moon

((

I'm fucking sick of hearing
people call me beautiful who
don't even know my middle
name,
When I'm too doubtful in
myself to take a compliment.
I'd much rather you be
intrigued by the thoughts
living inside my twisted
mind
Than the curvature of my
sides.

Friends With the

Moon

☾

I'd rather you have an effect
on the curvature of my spine,
Whether it be laughing or
gasping for air between the
sheets.
I need more than your sharp
jawline and bar drinks;
I need a whole lot of soul to
keep me at peace.

Friends With the Moon

☾

She's breathtaking and
powerful,
Like a natural disaster.
Winds blowing faster, waves
crashing;
So much beauty and chaos
wrapped up in her laughter.

Friends With the Moon

☾

Some say I'm poetic,
Some say I'm pretty;
But the ones who know me
best know—
That I have a dirty mind and
a dark sense of humor.
I love with the magnitude of
a category 1 storm.
I'm insane in the best of
ways, but who wants to be
sane, anyway?
I drink whiskey and I have a
filthy mouth.

Friends With the

Moon

☾

I'm intelligent and I'm
driven.
I stay lost in my own
thoughts most days.
I am a woman dreaming in
color,
Bleeding on paper.
I hope these words do
something for you.

Friends With the Moon

☽

My blood is boiling from the
warmth of your skin.
You make my spine curve
when your nails dig in.
That filthy mouth steals the
breath from my lungs and
etches pretty little marks
onto my shoulder.
Turn me over
And gag me for fun.
"That's a good girl."
I'm not *good* for just anyone.

Friends With the Moon

☾

I hope the next time you see
my face it steals your breath
away, like a bone-chilling
morning in the dead of
winter.

Friends With the Moon

☾

Imagine thinking you're only
capable of something as
useless as exterior beauty.
That, along with many other
things, will fade in time —
So please, my dear, strive to
be much more than *skin deep*.

Friends With the Moon

☾

There's a girl who once put
the sunshine in everything
she did.
In every word, and with every
smile she flashed;
Every touch
was beautifully contagious.
Effortlessly, she beamed with
brilliance.

Then one day, he sieged her
light

Friends With the Moon

☾

With ravenous, unwelcome
hands.
Leaving fingerprints she
wasn't able to wash off her
body.
She became no stranger to
heartache
And she nearly drowned in
oceans of tears,
As she mourned the loss of
herself.

Friends With the Moon

☾

But with this mourning,
eventually came strength.
She rose from her despair —
Unbroken by her tragedy,
Glowing with resilience.

Her light was long gone,
But now she shined with
something greater than
before—
Perseverance.
And a woman who
perseveres cannot be stopped

Friends With the

Moon

☾

By any man,
Or even an army of men.

Your tragedy did not break
you, my dear; it built you...
Into a force of nature.

Friends With the Moon

☾

Sometimes I wonder
How I'm so easy to let go of
By the hands that attempt to
hold me.
Perhaps, most hands are just
not built to hold the likes of
me;
For I hold many worlds
inside of me.
My soul is a terribly heavy
thing—

Friends With the Moon

☽

Bearing the magnitude of an
ocean, and I dare to say that
it's equally deep.

Friends With the Moon

☾

What is a mirror?

Is it the reflection of my body
dysmorphia?
Or perhaps, the reflection of
a narcissist's love for him or
herself?
Is it a reflected image of all
the atoms that collectively
make up the human standing
before it?
If our minds can alter these
images casting back and

Friends With the Moon

☾

distort reality, then what
good does a mirror do?

Fuck what you see, what do
you *feel*?

Do you love the soul which
lies within this capsule?
We must look beyond the
fine lines of wisdom under
our eyes and our love for
pasta, spilling over the brim
of our blue jeans.

Friends With the

Moon

☾

Imperfections make up a
unique, lovely piece of
artwork that is *you*.

You are 1/1.

And what you take with you
long after we're all gone is
not flesh and bones.

May a beautiful soul live on.

Friends With the

Moon

☾

You have much more
purpose in this life to fulfill
than seeking validation from
people who don't love you.

Friends With the Moon

Moon

☽

Look how swiftly those
watery eyes dried up, my
dear.
They are now smeared with
black—ready for war.

You can bring a woman to
her knees,
You can take away her rights,
You might even briefly tear
her down with your
distasteful words...
But this, I can promise you:

Friends With the

Moon

☾

When she rises up from the
ashes you will see that she is
not only powerful, but she
still remains delicate—much
like a flame.
This is when you will realize
that a woman is a force of
nature built by the Gods and
not something to conquer,
due to your fragile
masculinity.

Friends With the Moon

☾

Live a day in her skin.
Her cheeks are sunken in and
her spine holds up her flesh,
much like a circus tent.
Mommy's living with some
regrets after perceiving the
deeply-seeded thoughts she
planted inside that pretty
little head. Like weeds, they
grow to consume her just
overnight—in every crevice
of a young, impressionable
mind.

Friends With the Moon

☾

I'll plant seeds of all your
favorite flowers, in all the
colors you *so* love, under
those watery eyes. And when
the wells run dry the most
beautiful florets will surely
bloom, from the light that
shines from the inside out, in
you.

Live a day in her skin.
She's told that clothes are an
open invitation. Privilege

Friends With the Moon

☾

leads a man to think
everything is his for the
taking. What about the little
girl on the swingset in her
sundress? Forced entry,
leaves her stomach sinking,
when your monstrous hands
were never invited. Acting
like a "lady" won't save you,
for they prey on all shapes
and sizes.
So stand tall with your chest
out and dirty words all in

Friends With the Moon

☽

your mouth. Sitting pretty
with your lips sealed is not
what being a lady is about.

Live a day in her skin.
Bitterness stains her mind
just like the ink blots she
stares through, blankly.
"What do you see?"
Wrapped up in her own
mind, she's much too blinded
by the thoughts barging into
her head at all times; like a

Friends With the Moon

☾

runaway train, she can never

coax them long enough to get

some shut eye. Eat your pills

to heal your imbalanced

mind. Half-heartedly spilling

out your guts to strangers

when the safety of your walls

took years to build up so

high.

Put the pills down and look

at the woman in the mirror,

glowing with self-acceptance

and resilience. I hope you

Friends With the Moon

☾

know that between space and
time, that pretty little mind
was created, so divine. I
know it's hard when life
comes tumbling down on
your spine but pressure
makes diamonds. My love, I
see you shining.

Live a day in her skin.
Black and blue adorn her
wrists from shackles made by
his fingertips. She is a

Friends With the Moon

((

canvas; she is to be touched
gently, lovingly. May each
brush stroke of the hand be
full of purpose and good
intent.
The damage inhabiting her
mind far exceeds anything
that bruises or bleeds.
Alcohol drenched and ill
intent. Sleepless nights and
somber eyes, with weapons
hidden under your
pillowcase. She wakes to the

Friends With the Moon

☾

light seeping in each
morning but the nightmare is
still *so* unrelenting.
Women like you should be
nurtured the same way you
do. Heaven itself sent you as
proof—that angels walk
among us, too.

Every inch of you is different
from anyone, you're *1 of 1*.
You undoubtedly belong
upon grand, museum walls

Friends With the Moon

☾

with other pieces of priceless
art, like yourself. Tell them
you refuse to be another
clone; nobody ever fell in
love with life by trying to be
like everyone.

If the words from this piece
dressed you in chills: I am
writing this for you. If these
words felt foreign, I invite
you to live a day in her skin.

Friends With the Moon

☾

My dear,
You are enough—
Without emptying your
stomach after every meal,
Without your bones
protruding from your skin,
Without your cheeks, sunken
in.
You are perfectly made
And deserving of love.
You are—
So much more than *skin and
bones.*

Friends With the Moon

☾

Picket fence wrapped around
like a prison cell—
My own personal hell.
You fancy me in white, but
I'm no wife;
I'd rather marry the moon.
You'd like my lipstick spiked
with glue,
But my lips are drenched in
whiskey and they say what
they like.
Pretty and silent won't ever
suit me,

Friends With the Moon

☾

My tongue is sharp, like a
knife.

Friends With the Moon

☾

Prisoner of this body,
Ball and chain.
Mirror distorted like I'm at
the circus,
On the surface
I seem cool and collected
But in my head, it gets
Quite hectic and messy.
I'm a wreck.

Prisoner of my head,
Shackles on my ankles;
Overthinking,

Friends With the

Moon

☾

So much information
I'm still creating, when I'm
in my bed—
Sleep when I'm dead,
But I'm already deader than
the rest.
I just wanna rest.

Friends With the Moon

☾

May your love for yourself be
as deep as the sea.
For the abyss—the darkest
trenches of the earth and of
your mind—is where you will
find your self-worth.
Every beautiful warrior who
is in love with her own skin
has been deeply unhappy in
it, too.
I hope someday you learn to
love and embrace every scar
and stretch mark,

Friends With the Moon

((

for they leave you glowing

with growth and resilience.

-Things I tell the woman in

the mirror

Friends With the Moon

☽

Friends With the Moon

☾

The Ghosts of Lovers

Friends With the

Moon

☽

It was an honor to love
somebody like you.

Friends With the Moon

☾

I was drowning in words
From the moment your soul
found me out;
Could barely get them all
written down and
Still writing about—
You make for the best poetry,
whether you're making me
melt or bleeding me out.
Still have my note in the
window?
Sad that's all you have left of
me now,

Friends With the Moon

☾

I wish you'd rather grow old
with me
Than hang onto notes from
me,
But tragically,
We came apart at the seams.
I hope you know you haunt
me wide awake,
Not just in my dreams.
I didn't ask for a seance;
I'd rather be haunted by
Hemingway or some shit.
I'll admit—

Friends With the Moon

☾

I've been missing you for far
too long.
Come home,
It's hard to love you when
you're gone.

Friends With the Moon

☾

I wish I could unlove you,
like picking petals.
If only it was that easy to
pluck the heavily embedded
thoughts of you,
The words you said,
And the way you moved
every molecule in me
Right out of my sad, little
mind.
Maybe I'll tell myself sad
little lies,
Just to get me by.

Friends With the Moon

☾

I call him an artist.
He had a way of painting the
most intricately distorted
pictures,
In every color I so loved.
Painting me pretty little lies
with each brush stroke.
You're a goddamn Picasso,
aren't you?

Friends With the Moon

☽

I wish I could look at you as I
did before all the tragedy that
weighed upon us.
But now, when I look at you,
all I see are forest fires and
natural disasters;
Once beautiful, living, and
thriving things, dwindling
and dying off.
I see you as a shell of what
was once, inconceivably, a
home.

Friends With the Moon

☾

I'm glad you survived the
fire;
But I nearly burned you
down to ashes, didn't I?
These memories still linger,
but I can no longer live
suitably in the shell of a
human.

Friends With the Moon

☽

Today I thought about you,
and how
I resent the worn-in
bedsheets you woke up in;
I could embrace you with
better care.
I wonder what you'll be
sipping on to get you by
tonight, and I already envy
the bottle;
My lips are far more
inebriating, you see.

Friends With the Moon

☾

Oh, how I wish to be the
water in your shower after a
long day;
Honey, I could cleanse you
like no other.
But I suppose, for now, I'll
settle for being an evocative
afterthought—Existing
somewhere in the depths of
your mind, and hoping to
never fully be forgotten.

Friends With the Moon

☾

I have a love/hate
relationship with words.
Words have the power to give
me life and to haunt me, all
at once.
The words you gave to me
are all I have left of you, and
they resurface daily.
I replay them in my head
often; I'll admit, It's one of
my many faults.
I remember when you once
told me,

Friends With the Moon

☾

"You're the most colorful
person."

I wonder what colors you see
me in now, if any at all.
Perhaps, in your eyes, I am
now just etched with black
and white, and I will soon
become another stranger in a
crowded space that you won't
pay any mind.

Friends With the

Moon

☾

And yet, here you are... still
being made into my art.

Friends With the Moon

☽

I remember what a crazy fool
you made out of me.
It was only a matter of days
after we first met,
When I found myself singing
"At last" by Etta James;
My heart, exploding out of
my chest with the things I
felt for you
And still do...
But now all I can do is hum
ballads and look up at the
moon,

Friends With the Moon

(

wondering why he can't hold
the sun and why I can't hold
you.

Friends With the Moon

☽

I can no longer enjoy the call
of a train,
without the nostalgic
memories of you barging into
my brain.
-Haunted by the living

Friends With the Moon

☾

I thought we had it but then
we lost it.
Baby, I'm so exhausted.
I've tried every way in the
world to keep loving you, but
love's costing:
My sleep,
My dreams,
My self,
My peace.

This isn't love anymore.

Friends With the Moon

☽

He's a tall glass of water,
But he burns like whiskey
All the way down.
Just one taste and I—
Was utterly inebriated;
In your liquor
I'd gladly drown.

Friends With the

Moon

☾

Back arched, rising like the
sun.
I wrap myself around you
like a vine-
After only one glass of wine.
Dim the lights.
I'm lost in you,
Just give me one more night.

Friends With the

Moon

☾

Make love to my ears with
your breath.
Decorate them with
diamonds, made of sweet
nothings—
Shining with deception.
Leave me with words,
Rather than nothing,
When you steal my heart and
leave me for dead.

Friends With the Moon

☾

Wish you would stay, but I'm
used to you leaving;
So, I'll let go of my last hope,
and try to keep breathing.
Every day I can't taste you,
the taste is bitter.
I should've given up after 10
years, but I'm no quitter.
Say you don't know if this
whole thing's right,
So why'd we stay out all
night?

Friends With the Moon

☾

When I leave at dawn, I'll
wear an uneasy smile on my
face;
It'll drop like a dead match
soon as the door separates
us.

Friends With the Moon

☾

Out of all the nightmares,
And grotesque monsters,
And war,
And chaos that have haunted
me
And awoken me in my
slumber.

Out of the numerous times
I've come to, with chills—
My heart pounding,
Unable to catch my breath...
I must confess—

Friends With the Moon

☾

That the most terrifying,
daunting
And unsettling dream I've
yet to wake from in my
entirety
Is the one in which:

I'm holding your face, like
I'm holding the world,
Right at my fingertips
Tracing every edge of you
Astonished and consumed,
even

Friends With the Moon

☾

Marveling how people like
you exist
Getting lost in your
dark-eyed gaze
The utterance of ardor and
relief escape your tongue
Confessing how you've
craved me all these years—
How we never have to long
for one another again
My heart is content

Only to wake, alone

Friends With the Moon

☾

In an empty, despairing sea

of sheets

In a reality in which,

You no longer love me.

-Unrequited

Friends With the Moon

☾

You were warm and you were
safe but he was *fire*—
An angel's face with a
devilish smile.

Friends With the Moon

☾

...Won't you save me the last dance?

Friends With the Moon

☾

I still remember the way your
fingertips used to trickle
down the curve of my spine,
Like a calm rain gracing the
window pane after a
hellacious storm.

Friends With the Moon

☽

I hope you find more beauty
to life than just in shiny
things,
And I hope you realize I was
much more than just *that*.

Friends With the Moon

☾

Nostalgia: a reminder that after all, time machines *do* exist.

Friends With the

Moon

☾

You'll never forget what it
felt like to be loved by me.

Friends With the

Moon

☾

Friends With the

Moon

☾

Moon Thoughts

Friends With the Moon

☾

I'm afraid the only escape
we have in this life lies
within each other and in art.

Friends With the

Moon

☾

Don't get me all wrong, many
captivating love stories have
come and gone.
But in my opinion, the best
art is inspired by either
sadness or madness.

Friends With the Moon

☾

My greatest downfall and my
greatest attribute, I'm afraid,
is that I can look into the
eyes of a monster and still
find something worth loving.

Friends With the Moon

☾

I can feel myself withering
away, much like the end of a
cigarette.
The clock ticks
unrelentingly,
And I am drowning tonight.
Meet me in the depths,
where time goes to die
And clocks tend to melt.

Friends With the Moon

☾

Can you blame me... that I've
always been captivated by
fire?
The burn entices me: a
masochist.
Always leaving a mark on my
flesh that allows no room for
disregard.
Forever captivated by the
way the flame forced
surrender with just one
effortless caress.

Friends With the Moon

☾

I hope the incessant thought
of me is caught up
somewhere between your
daydreams and your
nightmares.

Friends With the

Moon

☾

I'm sorry about all the nights
you stay wide awake,
With heavy eyes.
Searching desperately for a
sign,
That someone feels the same
as you do.
That feeling of longing—
Fear of the unknown.
Searching for songs and
scripture and anything to put
your mind at ease;

Friends With the Moon

☽

To help you know you are
not alone.
Well, the truth is —
We're all a little broken,
And we're all a little mad.

Friends With the Moon

☾

Have I died or am I still
alive?
Coherent but demented,
Cold but on fire,
Jekyll and Hyde,
Sharp edges, like a knife.
A walking paradox or a sick
fuck who's off their rocker?
You tell me.

The room is spinning and
any memory leading up to

Friends With the Moon

☾

this very minute is but a blur
in time.
My extremities are numb,
and my chest feels much like
a hollow, distressed vase
which gives home to the
half-dead flowers that make
up my crippled mind.

My mind is a mess just like
the hair on my head, and the
things going on inside would

Friends With the

Moon

☾

surely frighten you, so I'll
keep them to myself.

Drown me in your holy
water.
Hide your sons and hide your
daughters.
The undead is no longer at
rest.
-Birth of A Zombie

Friends With the Moon

☾

Sometimes all we can do
Is drown out these racing
thoughts with pretty noise
and strange cartoons.
How lucky we are to have
artists
To soothe our souls from a
distance,
When all else we have is the
moon.

Friends With the Moon

☾

Be careful with your
thoughts; perspective is
everything.
Four walls make both a home
and a prison cell.

Friends With the

Moon

☾

When most people's eyes
become fixated on the night
sky, they are often captivated
by the seemingly miniscule
glimmers that are entrapped
worlds beyond what we could
fathom.
I, however, find the vast sea
of darkness that threatens to
nearly swallow me whole,
entirely more mesmerizing.

Friends With the Moon

☽

She feels uneasy, stomach
sinking, her restless jaw
grinds.
The numbness has come and
gone and so grows her desire.
A shiver dances up her bony
little spine.
Always scheming for another
line.
What's it like to live only for
the next high?

Friends With the Moon

☾

Beautiful girl, bright red lips,
but her cheeks are sunken in
and she's dead in the eyes.
Skin crawling;
When's the last time you had
a bite?
-Girl across the bar

Friends With the

Moon

☾

He looked into the face of
death as she smirked at him,
sending chills down his skin
with the slightest caress.
Crimson red lips drew him
in.
His spine tightened.
He asked her for a dance and
she smiled with a sinful grin.
-Dancing with Death

Friends With the Moon

☾

"The American Dream" is
but a ruse;
You tighten your black tie
like a noose.
You sell your soul for some
fools gold, when you should
be searching for soul food.

Friends With the Moon

☾

Be particularly careful when
choosing the words you say
to a writer.
For those very words will live
on
in the depths of a writer's
mind,
Being replayed, as if on an
old tape recorder—
For much longer than you
could fathom.

Friends With the Moon

☽

These words you say,
sometimes we drown in
them;
These words you say,
sometimes they swallow us
whole.

Friends With the Moon

Moon

☾

There's nothing like the
quiet nights I spend alone,
Sipping whiskey and
bleeding words.

Friends With the Moon

☾

Friends With the Moon

☾

The Sun Will Shine

Again

Friends With the

Moon

☾

She is one with the sun,
friends with the moon.
If you've the luck to
encounter her, you will see
that—
She, too, controls the violent
tides that drown and she, too,
beams with brilliance—
giving life to the Earth
around you.

Friends With the Moon

☾

You, my dear, are as deep as
the ocean.
There are many who will
admire your alluring waves
from afar but are fearful of
drowning in your depths.
Many will dip their toes with
no intention of being fully
submerged in the vast beauty
that is *you*.

Friends With the

Moon

☾

Perhaps one day our society
will start measuring the
health progressions of bodies
with more than just a
measuring tape.

Friends With the Moon

☽

Long after I'm gone you
should know, you haven't
seen the last of me.
Oh, no -
Long after the remnants of
what my bones may give to
the soil is embraced by the
Earth, the smallest seed with
infinite hope will nestle
comfortably into the ground
where I last laid, and bloom
slowly into a lovely, delicate
floral friend.

Friends With the Moon

☾

And all those who find
beauty in the most simple
things will smile as they
witness me embracing the
sweet rays the sun gives so
generously.
I will soon gain the strength
from the nutrients my roots
seek, to bloom and give life
to my frequent visitors: the
bees.
From my pollen they will
produce sweet, golden honey.

Friends With the Moon

☾

Life is restored.

Friends With the Moon

☾

Baby girl, fifteen, spitting
image of me.
Growing up seeing things
little girls shouldn't see.
I know you worry when you
see mommy looking back in
the mirror.
But it's not in you, love.
You're destined for
greatness.
You don't know why she
couldn't choose you over the
illness.

Friends With the Moon

Moon

☾

But the truth is, sometimes
people fall apart.
Sometimes we just need to
find forgiveness in our
hearts.
Don't get me wrong, I know
you'll never forget—
All the nights you spent
going to war in your head.
But it's not worth the
anguish, so just let the love
fill your heart instead.

Friends With the

Moon

☽

'Cause we weren't meant to
be perfect, we were meant to
be *art*.

Friends With the Moon

☾

May each step you take be
filled with divine purpose,
my love.
May every man you meet
weep at your knees,
overwhelmed by your divine
femininity, though their
validation you'll ever need.
When you tremble with fear
just know I'll be there;
there's no secret you could
utter to make me unlove you.

Friends With the Moon

☾

You mustn't forget you are
perfectly made, no matter
what size or shape.
You'll live a lifetime of
mistakes that teach you every
step of the way, that life is
not about wading...
You must dive deep to
discover the vast beauty of
what lies beneath the
surface.

Friends With the Moon

☾

Mommy always told you to
be polite.
Daddy preached, "boys don't
cry."
All your life you struggle to
understand,
What it means to be a man.
The media tells you that
women and wealth
Will make you feel your
fullest self.
Stand up taller, button your
collar,

Friends With the Moon

☾

Swallow some pills to numb
the feels,
Because that's how to "be a
man."
You've grown so numb to
this life you lead,
When the drugs wear off you
sit and bleed
Wondering who you're living
for.
Tears escape your eyes and
drop like bombs on the floor;

Friends With the Moon

☽

Your head and your heart at
war.
You're a man, but you're so
much more.
-Boys don't cry

Friends With the

Moon

☾

My words cannot give you
the will to live—
This, I know.
But I also know for certain,
since you're reading this
passage, that it's still deeply
embedded inside of you;
perhaps, it is curled up under
your rib cage next to your
half-dead heart, and I am
determined to pry it out from
its place of hiding.

Friends With the Moon

☽

Every time you rested the
cold barrel on your temple
but didn't blow out your
mental, don't you wonder
why?
Why aren't you dead and
buried like you thought you
would be by now?
Every day the mirror casts
back a pale and colorless
corpse haunting you
inconspicuously.

Friends With the Moon

☾

But it's no ghost—only the
ghost of a girl who once lived
her life in vibrant hues,
choking on her very own
laughter.
She's the one who's dead and
buried now.
All that's left is this empty
shell of a human wandering
around mindlessly in search
of some form of fulfillment
or happiness.

Friends With the

Moon

☽

The thing is, you see, you
still have much left to do
here.
You have lives to touch and
ripples of hope in humanity
to spread far and wide.
Can't you see?
There are people who need to
feel your love and they want
to drown you endlessly in
their love for you with all the
same efforts.

Friends With the

Moon

☾

There are strong young women and men you've yet to give birth to with your bulletproof, beautifully crafted body. My love, only you can raise them to breathe fire and fight like vikings in this relentless game of life. When the ones who raised you grow old and withered like a rose, don't you wish to return the favor when comes the reverse of roles?

Friends With the

Moon

☾

But most importantly, do not
forget this:
Between space and
time—that pretty little mind
was created, so divine.
There's a fire inside you, one
you must not let die.
You have not fought every
day since the beginning of
your existence and crossed
oceans of fear and
forgiveness to *surrender*.

Friends With the

Moon

☾

-The gunshot that refused

you

Friends With the Moon

☾

I used to think that love
meant hanging onto
something for dear life;
clinging to them like you
have nothing else to live for.
But love, I have found, is
letting go.
Not to suffocate them in the
depths, but to help them stay
afloat.

Friends With the Moon

☾

May the sun always be a
perfect representation of
love:
Holding the power to end all
of humanity—yet,
She is merciful.
She chooses to give life,
instead.

Friends With the Moon

☽

Don't forget about those who
loved you on your darkest
days, when your soul was
sinking into your spine.
When the contents of the
bottle were all that got you
through each fragile day that
passed by.
When it took all the energy
mustered up inside of you to
wear a fabricated smile.
Please don't forget who
stayed by your side—

Friends With the Moon

☾

Who kept you safe.
Don't forget me.

Friends With the

Moon

☾

Baby, why would you jump
when you don't have wings
just *yet*?
Know it's easy to get caught
up inside that pretty head,
Thinking you're better off
dead.
But you're different from the
rest of us.

Won't you just stay?
Can't you see, the world is
begging you to stay?

Friends With the Moon

☾

I'm begging you to stay.

It would be one hell of a
lonely world without the sun,
One hell of a lonely world
without you.

And you should know—
The sun bleeds sometimes,
too.

Friends With the Moon

☾

She's one hell of a woman,
Her laugh is infectious.
When she smiles her soul
shines so bright
that flowers bloom in her
direction.

Friends With the Moon

☾

Tell your sister you love her.
Tell her you love her, even
when she's heartache and
shipwreck—
Especially then.
Tell her you've always
admired her for the things
she bears, that you lack.
Tell her she has the most
soul-stealing eyes that have
graced the planet.
Tell her you write about her
often,

Friends With the Moon

☽

And that the pages are
covered in stardust each time
you do.

Friends With the

Moon

☾

My dear, I have learned that
some of the most beautiful
things to be experienced in
this life stretch far beyond
what the mind could fashion
into mere words.
And one of those few things,
indeed, is you.

Friends With the Moon

☾

I've seen more love prosper
inside prison walls than I've
ever seen at an altar.
I've seen the weight of the
world be carried on a young
woman's shoulders.
She was sure all the watery
eyes and soul-stirring nights
would kill her slowly.
But with each day the tears
subsided, and she became
nothing short of a warrior.

Friends With the Moon

☾

Flowers bloomed under her
somber eyes following all the
rain and doubt.
Her soul, it shines from the
inside out.
The devil tried to
compromise her sweet smile
but had no luck.
She is a lighthouse standing
tall,
A monument of unwavering
hope.

Friends With the Moon

☾

Guiding him safely from the
storm that outbroke.
Her love for him, it will not
falter.
What more could a father
want in a daughter?
She never knew the weight of
the world would mold her
into a diamond.
Keep that head up baby girl,
The way you shine is
blinding.

Friends With the

Moon

☽

I pray every day that angels
keep you safe.

Friends With the Moon

((

The will to live: something,
sadly, you cannot give.
I watched the color fade
right out of your skin like
dilute ink.
I watched you cease to exist
before your body was ready
to be submerged into the
Earth.
Always believing you must
live up to others'
expectations; going to war in
your own mind relentlessly.

Friends With the

Moon

☾

The mind is a powerful
thing.
We speak about weapons of
mass destruction, but never
about the one resting behind
your very own eyes.
Put your weapon down
And I will plant flowers
under those watery eyes,
In every color you adore.
It will only be a matter of
time until they bloom, dear.
-I hope these words save you

Friends With the Moon

☾

I write these incandescent combinations of words to soothe my uneasy soul when my mind won't allow for much sleep; and if you're reading this, I write to soothe yours all the same.

Friends With the Moon

☾

Friends With the Moon

☽

Friends With the

Moon

☾